John Horne Tooke

A Letter to a Friend on the Reported Marriage of His Royal Highness the Prince of Wales

John Horne Tooke

A Letter to a Friend on the Reported Marriage of His Royal Highness the Prince of Wales

ISBN/EAN: 9783337329327

Printed in Europe, USA, Canada, Australia, Japan

Cover: Foto ©ninafisch / pixelio.de

More available books at **www.hansebooks.com**

A

LETTER

TO A

RIEND,

ON THE

REPORTED MARRIAGE

OF HIS ROYAL HIGHNESS THE

RINCE OF WALES.

By Mr. HORNE TOOKE.

THE SECOND EDITION.

———————

LONDON:

PRINTED FOR J. JOHNSON, N° 72, ST. PAUL'S
CHURCH-YARD.

M.DCC.LXXXVII.

A

LETTER

TO A

FRIEND, &c.

April 1787.

YOU agree intirely with me then, that the queſtion will be blinked on both ſides; and that a ſincere performance of their duty, either to his majeſty on the one hand, or to his royal highneſs on the other, is not reaſonably to be expected from either Party : that thoſe who are IN, conforming juſt ſo far as may be

B   neceſſary

neceffary to keep them *in*, will yet be in-
dividually very cautious not to exclude
themfelves hereafter : and that thofe who
are OUT, though careful not to forfeit
their future expectations, will yet by no
means be contented to wàit for that diftant
and uncertain period ; and, by a faithful
adherence to his royal highnefs, fhut the
door againft themfelves to nearer (and
therefore dearer) contingencies and advan-
tages. In fhort, that both the INS and
the OUTS are moft accurate and ready cal-
culators of the refpective and comparative
value of a prefent and a reverfionary benefit ; and will regulate their conduct ac-
cordingly.

Meafured therefore, and regardful of
this double profpect, as will be the language of all the Parties on this queftion ;
you agree with me that it is not from the
debates

debates of either houfe of parliament that the public will receive any folid or ufeful information on a point of fo much importance to the nation, to the fovereign on the throne, to his royal fucceffor, and to a moft amiable and juftly valued female character, whom I conclude to be in all refpects, both *legally*, really, worthily, and *happily for this country*, her royal highnefs the Princefs of Wales.

The aftonifhment and oppofition which this conclufion of mine excited at the firft declaration to you of my fentiments on this marriage, removes from my mind all fufpicion of complaifance in the fatisfaction and conviction which you profefs to have received from my arguments : and I yield with lefs reluctance to your folicitation thus publicly to exhibit them to others.

　　　　　　　There

'There might perhaps be a proper deli‐ cacy before, and an individual might rea‐ fonably be unwilling to put his fickle in‐ to the corn before the harveft was ready; but after the fhameful pamphlets we have feen *, (*fhameful,* becaufe on *both* fides unjuft to the prince of Wales and cruel to a defencelefs woman), and after the con‐ verfations which have been held in the houfe of commons and publifhed in all the news-papers, together with the dif‐ courfe which has circulated univerfally through the nation; it would be a moft ridiculous affectation to hefitate in fo many words to declare, that it is reported (and by me on folid grounds believed) that his royal highnefs the prince of Wales is mar‐ ried to the late Mrs. Fitzherbert.

---

* See *A fhort Review of the political State of Great-Britain.* And *The People's Anfwer to the Court Pamphlet,* &c.

Whilft

Whilft this meafure was yet in contemplation, it was known to me on good authority. I thought of it and fpoke of it then, as I think and fpeak now; and therefore earneftly wifhed and had much joy in its completion.

For what reafon, in the name of God, (except for their own interefted reafons) have the profeffed friends of his royal highnefs ftood aloof; and affected to keep it fecret, or to difbelieve it? When both his honour and his *intereft*, and her honour, and their own, fhould have urged them to make it as authentic and as public as poffible.

But fuch a marriage, it is faid, is generally held to be both highly *improper* *,

and

---

* There is no end of fanciful and foolifh improprieties. One fet of very pious chriftians held it highly

improper,

and *legally impoſſible*. And both theſe no-
tions have been countenanced by the ſhy-
neſs of his royal highneſs's profeſſed
friends, and have been ſuffered to take too
deep a root in the minds of the uninform-
ed part of the public.

'Tis true. It has been held *improper.*
But there are political as well as religious
ſuperſtitions *. Ghoſts, phantoms, hob-
goblins of every denomination, have at different

---

improper, that a woman ſhould undergo the marriage
ceremony any otherwiſe than with her hair diſhevelled :
and for this dreadful *impropriety* they quarrelled very
ſeriouſly with another ſet of chriſtians, altogether as
pious as themſelves, who thought it quite ſufficient if
her hair was diſhevelled afterwards.

* About two hundred and ſixty years ago, ſome
gentlemen of the *Païs de Vaud*, eating their ſoup haſtily
with *wooden* ſpoons, undoubtedly ſhewed their judgment

ferent periods been raifed by interefted, fometimes by felf-deceiving forcerers, be-fetting and difmaying with panic terrors the yielding and too fufceptible imagina-tions of men.

Improper: becaufe Mrs. Fitzherbert was an Englifh fubject, and not defcended from a *fovereign* houfe. And *legally impoffible:*

---

ment and good fenfe, in declaring them more *proper* for that purpofe than metal fpoons, as not retaining the heat and burning their mouths like the latter. But they are not much to be praifed for inftituting an *order* of the fpoon, and endeavouring to inforce this *propriety* by waging a bloody and tedious war with their neigh-bours, to compel them to ufe the fame. Yet, whim-fical as it may appear, the reader may find in Jacob Spon's *Hiftoire de Geneve*, Tom. I. page 320, that thefe *knights of the fpoon*, who wore it as an honourable badge round their necks, were not finally fubdued but by a regular allied army from Berne, Fribourg, Soleure, and Geneva, amounting to twelve thoufand men, with eighteen pieces of cannon.

be-

becaufe there is an act of parliament in the way.

They however who affect to be fhocked at this impropriety, muft either know very little, or moft grofsly diffemble the little which they know of the hiftory of their country. To match in marriage with a fubject was, at all times within memory, a common and well-precedented practice of the fovereigns of this realm: nor was it ever interrupted down to the very acceffion of the prefent family on the throne. — Only feventy-three years ago. The two immediate predeceffors of George the Firft, being themfelves (as well as our great Elizabeth) the iffue of fuch a match. Not only fo, but the Houfe of Stuart itfelf, which immediately preceded the Houfe of Hanover, and the very fove-reign under whom the Houfe of Hano-

5

ver claims, being the iſſue of ſuch a match. The race of Tudor alſo, which immediately preceded that of Stuart, and the very ſovereign under whom the Houſe of Stuart claims, being the iſſue of ſuch a match. *Three* out of *Six* ſovereigns of the Houſe of Stuart, and *Three* out of *Five* ſovereigns of the Houſe of Tudor, were the iſſue of ſuch matches. So that the *majority*, for a courſe of two hundred and thirty years, namely, *Six* out of the *Eleven* ſovereigns, immediately preceding the Houſe of Hanover, were the iſſue of ſuch matches.

Nor did any miſchief ever ariſe to this country; nor, if examined fairly, will it appear probable that any miſchief ever ſhould ariſe from ſuch a practice. On the contrary, the greateſt miſchiefs may be ſhewn at all times and in all countries

to

to have arifen from the oppofite practice. Such mifchief, for inftance, as arofe from the marriages of Maximilian with the daughter of Charles Duke of Burgundy; and of his fon Philip with the daughter of Ferdinand and Ifabella: which convulfed all Europe for centuries; and of which the Dutch, even at this day, ftill feel the fatal confequences.

This degrading notion of impropriety, and that a beautiful Englifh woman is unworthy to be the companion of an Englifh prince, is a ridiculous phantom imported into this land only with the Houfe of Hanover *: to whom indeed it was formerly

---

* Charles the Second had no notion of fuch a prejudice, and gave no other reafon for not marrying one of his own fubjects, than that he had not feen any one of them whom he liked well enough.—" The Chan-
" cellor

merly no phantom, but a ferious and well-founded confideration. For by the Ger-

---

" cellor afked him; whether his majefty had given
" over all thoughts of a proteftant wife? To which
" he anfwered; He could find none fuch, except
" amongft his own fubjects, and amongft them he had
" feen none that pleafed him enough to that end."
Continuation of the Life of Edward Earl of Clarendon. Vol. 2. page 149. But his true motive appears
plainly to have been, that his majefty, (in conformity
both with his fituation and character) meant merely to
make a Smithfield bargain; and none of his own fubjects were able to bring him fuch a portion as was offered with the Infanta of Portugal, viz. five hundred
thoufand pounds fterling, with the addition of three
hundred thoufand piftoles from France. His marriage
and the fale of Dunkirk proceeded from the fame motive: His carcafe and the town were furrendered on
the fame conditions. And in regard to the latter,
Lord Clarendon tells us—" There remained no other
" queftion, than into what hand to put it. And the
" meafure of that was only who would give moft
" money for it, there being no inclination to prefer
" one before another."

But

Germanic confederacy, which may truly and properly be ſtyled a republic of princes, the law of ſucceſſion in Germany has been ſettled in the true ſpirit of ſuch a republic; which conſidered merely, in all its acts, the excluſive intereſts of its legiſlating ſovereigns, with a moſt royal

---

But to be ſatisfied of the novelty of the prejudice, the reader has only to recollect—That Henry the Seventh was the deſcendant of a marriage with a ſubject: His ſon Henry the Eighth married *four* of his ſubjects. Edward the Sixth was the iſſue of ſuch a marriage. Queen Elizabeth was the iſſue of ſuch a marriage. Mary Queen of Scots married a ſubject. James the Firſt was the iſſue of ſuch a marriage. His grandſon Charles the Second had no prejudice againſt ſuch a marriage. His brother James the Second married a ſubject. Queen Mary and Queen Anne were the iſſue of ſuch a marriage. George the Firſt married the daughter of ſuch a marriage. George the Second was the grandſon of ſuch a marriage. Leaving the people therefore out of the queſtion, if we ſeek for this prejudice, where it was moſt likely to inhabit, in the breaſts of our ſovereigns; we ſhall not find, from

difregard and contempt of the fubject *.
By that law indeed the iffue of an unequal
match

---

from the reign of Richard the Third down to his prefent majefty, any one who could poffibly have given it
harbour, except indeed the two deteftable characters,
Queen Mary and Charles the Firft.

* The juftice of this reflexion may poffibly be difputed; becaufe the antient and conftitutional law of
the empire fays—" Les mêmes loix qui dans l'empire
" reglent les droits des princes, font celles qui reglent
" ceux des particuliers: elles font également facrées,
" foit qu'elles étendent, foit qu'elles bornent l'autorité
" des uns et la fujettion des autres." Now this is
very well faid. But the conduct of the Electors in the
fubfequent capitulations by which they bind the empe-
ror, and the practices which have obtained, correfpond
too literally with that *fpirit* which I have imputed to
them. For " autrefois il n'y avoit point de princi-
" pauté qui n'eut des états provinciaux, et les feigneurs
" étoient obligés de les confulter dans les affaires les
" plus importantes du gouvernement et de l'admini-
" ftration. Aujourd'hui ils font abolis en plufieurs
" endroits."

" Suivant

match (as it is abfurdly and arrogantly ftyled) viz. of a fovereign with a confort not defcended of a fovereign houfe; all

---

" Suivant le dernier réces de l'empire, les cours
" fouveraines ne doivent pas recevoir facilement les
" actions des fujets contre leurs fuperieurs, et avant de
" le faire elles doivent écrire à ceux-ci pour leur de-
" mander des eclairciffements."

" L'empereur fera toujours fentir aux fujets l'obeif-
" fance qu'ils doivent à leurs feigneurs."

" Il eft permis aux Electeurs, princes et états de
" l'empire de fe maintenir contre leurs fujets et avec
" l'affiftance de leurs voifins, et de les forcer à l'obeif-
" fance."

" Les feigneurs territoriaux peuvent à bon droit ôter
" aujourd'hui à leurs fujets *l'ancienne liberté allemande,*
" qui confiftoit à aller fervir chez les puiffances étran-
" geres."

Had this laft ufurpation amounted to a total prohibition, inftead of a transfer of this favage right, no
friend of humanity would have complained. But we
faw in the late American war, that, inftead of felling
themfelves, the fovereigns by formal bargain and fale
received the price of their fubjects blood : therein ex-
ceeding infinitely the reproach of Vefpafian, who only
took a profit on their urine.

I

iffue

iſſue of ſuch a match is barred the ſuccef-
ſion in .Germany. So, at this preſent
period, the children by an unequal match
of Prince Louis of Wirtemberg, eldeſt
nephew of the reigning Duke, will be ſet
aſide ; and the iſſue of a younger branch
ſucceed *. An Electⁿ of Hanover had
there-

* " Pour ſucceder à un territoire, il faut néceſſaire-
" ment être d'une naiſſance proportionée à la dignité
" d'Etat ; parceque, ſuivant l'ancien droit Allemand,
" un enfant doit être d'une naiſſance égale des deux
" côtés, et ſuit toûjours la pire main. Un mariage
" égal et convenable pour un etat, eſt celui qu'un
" prince ou comte contracte avec une perſonne de la
" haute nobleſſe. Une mes-alliance ou mariage in-
" égale, eſt celui qui ſe fait entre la haute et la baſſe
" nobleſſe, ou entre nobles ſeigneurs et miniſteriaux
" (Knechtſtand.)" Tableau du gouvernement actuel
de l'empire d'Allemagne. 1755. pag. 313.
The French tranſlator of Profeſſor Schmaufs, aſſerts
in his advertiſement, that this German cuſtom ſprings
from the erroneous extenſion and application of an an-
cient

therefore good reafon to be cautious by his marriage to preferve the Electorate to his pofterity. But when the fovereignty of Hanover and of the kingdoms of Great-Britain and Ireland became vefted in one perfon; (which is precifely the period when this ridiculous notion of impropriety commenced in this kingdom); it became the intereft of the fubjects of Great-Britain (and of Hanover too: for the union is moft undoubtedly prejudicial to both), inftead of adopting this new

---

cient law of Charlemagne: for that, in point of marriage, there is no real inequality of conditions, except only between the conditions of fiee and flave: " d'où " l'on doit conclure (fays the tranflator) qu'il n'y au- " roit point de mes-alliance entre un empereur et la " fille d'un de ces gentils hommes que les Allemans ap- " pellent *Freyhern*." If fuch be the liberal opinion of a Frenchman, with what contempt fhould an Englifh gentleman treat this " *High-Dutch ignorance and* " *pride*."

and

d degrading prejudice, moſt anxiouſly to
ke advantage of the only poſſible means
a peaceful ſeparation, which this very
w of the ſucceſſion in Germany af-
rded.

From the acceſſion therefore of the
Houſe of Hanover to this realm, ſuch a
marriage (however indifferent before) be-
ame not only *not improper*, but moſt de-
outly to be wiſhed for by the ſubjects of
Great-Britain and Hanover : and the ſove-
eign or the prince, who ſhall patriotically,
or the happineſs of both dominions, ſe-
arate this foreign poſſeſſion from his ſuc-
eſſor on the throne of Great-Britain *, will
deſerve

---

* It ſhould ſeem alſo particularly honourable and
appy for his majeſty, that ſuch an event ſhould take
place at this time rather than any other ; as it would,
by an eaſy arrangement, afford the immediate oppor-

tunity

deferve additional gratitude and an additional blefling from both. And although, as I can eafily believe, it might happen, that a lefs noble but more amiable motive fhould produce this eligible feparation ; the effect and benefit being the fame, we fhould only transfer that additional gratitude and blefling, where we fhould owe the obligation, to Englifh beauty and merit. Such an event, to render it completely beneficial, would leave us nothing to pray for, but for an offspring by fuch a marriage.

But by an Act of Parliament, 12 Geo. III. fuch a marriage (whether proper and

---

tunity of a proper eftablifhment for another branch of his majefty's family ; and he would himfelf, without any diminution, expence, or coft, enjoy the fatisfaction and glory of a fecond race of fovereigns defcending alfo from his loins.

beneficial,

beneficial, or otherwife) is faid *now* to be *legally* impoffible: for that act recites—

" That no defcendant of the body of his
" late majefty king George the Second *,
" male or female (other than the iffue of
" *princeffes*, who have married or may
" hereafter marry into foreign families)
" fhall be *capable of contracting matri-*
" *mony*, without the previous confent of
" his majefty, his heirs or fucceffors, fig-
" nified under the great feal, and declared

---

* How little could *Mifs D'Olbreufe*, a young French lady of equal beauty and merit perhaps, but in no refpect fuperior to, if of equal condition with Mrs. Fitzher-bert; how little could fhe forefee that a precedent would, in no very diftant time, be attempted for vio-lating the deareft and moft effential rights of mankind, in order to guard *her* pofterity from fuch a marriage as that to which they owe their exiftence ! But fuch is the fact : for our late juft and excellent king, George the Second, was himfelf the grandfon of Mifs D'Ol-breufe.

in

" in council; and that every marriage or
" matrimonial contract of any such de-
" scendant, without such consent first
" had and obtained, shall be *null* and *void*
" to all intents and purposes whatsoever.
" Provided always, that in case any such
" descendant of the body of his late ma-
" jesty king George the Second, *being*
" *above the age of twenty-five years*, shall
" *persist* in his or her resolution to con-
" tract a marriage disapproved of or dis-
" sented from by the king, his heirs or
" successors; that then such descendant,
" upon giving notice to the king's privy-
" council, may at any time, from the
" expiration of twelve calendar months
" after such notice given to the council
" as aforesaid, contract such marriage;
" and his or her marriage with the per-
" son before proposed and rejected may
" be duly solemnized without the pre-

" vious

" vious confent of his Majefty, his heirs
" or fucceffors : and fuch marriage fhall
" be good, as if this act had never been
" made, UNLESS both houfes of parlia-
" ment fhall before the expiration of the
" faid twelve months exprefsly declare
" *their* difapprobation of fuch intended
" marriage."

Now I acknowledge this to be an act
of parliament ; but I deny it to have the
fmalleft force of law *. The antient
education

---

* A common reader will be furprized perhaps at
hearing, that there are Acts of parliament which are
not Laws. I remember an act, paffed but a few years
fince, which directed the juftices of the peace to take
forty fhillings out of twenty. Let the reader afk himfelf—Could this act be a Law ?

" It appeareth in our books, that in many cafes the
" Common Law doth controul acts of parliament, and

" fome-

education of our noblemen and gentlemen (of whom our parliaments were formerly compofed) imbuing them with the
principles of law, and the confequent wife
acts of our anceftors having always infured
obedience; I do not much wonder that
there fhould now be found perfons of a
very different defcription and education
(from the ftable, the nurfery, the gaming-
houfe and the counting-houfe) who abfurdly imagine that they have only to pafs
an Act, and that fuch act of parliament
will, or ought, or can, bind the fubject *in*

" fometimes fhall adjudge them to be void: for when
" an act of parliament is againft common right and
" reafon, or repugnant or impoffible to be performed,
" the common law fhall controul it, and adjudge fuch
" act to be void."—" Some ftatutes are made againft
" common law and right, which thofe who made them
" would not put in execution," &c. &c. Lord Coke
in Bonham's Cafe.

all

all cafes whatfoever. The laws of God indeed are as extenfive and illimitable as his nature: but as all things human are bounded, fo the objects and effects of human laws have their limits. This act of parliament trangreffes them, and is *null:* for though Law may regulate the exercife of our natural rights, it cannot totally take them away. If every common attorney knows that you cannot even leafe a pump to a tenant, and by any form of words reftrain him from drawing the water; what reafonable or juft conftruction muft a Judge, according to the law, his oath, or confcience, give to an act of parliament which fhould attempt to empower a parent who had begotten a child with the organs of fpeech, to tie up the child's tongue, and reftrain his articulation; until that parent fhould confent to take off the interdiction, and permit him the ufe of

language ?

language? Or until the fon fhould have more intereft with parliament than his father, and obtain (perhaps at *fixty*) *their* permiffion, without the father's confent, to enjoy the common diftinction of a human being? What conftruction, I afk, muft a judge give to a fimilar act of parliament, reftraining eye-fight, or eating, or digeftion?

For my own part, I can more eafily believe, that thofe with whom his majefty advifed for the paffing of this act, were willing to deceive him with the falfe femblance of a law *, than that they were them-

---

* This fuppofition will not appear fo very extraordinary to thofe who recollect a trick of the fame kind, in the fifth year of his majefty's reign; when his minifters, defirous of appearing to have empowered him, in cafe of a minority, to appoint as Regent her late royal

themselves deceived. For, knowing none
of that description, I will not without
proof believe, that there exist in this
country any persons so base as to advise or
to assist a parent to degrade his children to
something worse than castration, to the
unmanly state and abject condition of a

---

royal highness the princess dowager of Wales, but
without the mention of her name, which at that time
was not the most popular; they passed a bill with some
difficulty through the Commons; to empower his majesty to appoint as Regent ANY ONE of his royal family.
The trick was however discovered by a question (if I
mistake not, of the late Duke of Bedford) to the judges
in the House of Lords : for their answer determined, that
his majesty's mother was no part of his family. And
in order to prevent her exclusion, which would other-
wise have been the case, it became necessary to unmask
the intention, and to insert in the act the princess
dowager by name.

Friar ;

Friar *; and to compel them by an unnatural law, *without any fixed period*, to a
life of forced celibacy, until—(or rather
UNLESS) himfelf, like the pope, fhall be
pleafed to grant a difpenfation to reftore
them to the dignity of manhood, and re-

- * The oldeft charter extant, by which a prince of
Wales was formerly created, declares very different
and much more worthy views and fentiments.

    " De ferenitate regalis præeminentiæ, velut ex fole
" radii, fic inferiores prodeunt principatus, ut regiæ
" claritatis integritas de luce lucem proferens, ex
" lucis diftributione minoratæ lucis non fentiat detri-
" menta : immo tanto magis regale fceptrum extol-
" litur et folium regium fublimatur, quanto tribunali
" fuo plures fubfunt proceres eminenciæ clarioris.
" Hæc autem confideratio condigna nos, qui nominis
" et honoris primogeniti noftri chariffimi incremen-
" tum appetimus, alicit et inducit ut ipfum, *qui repu-*
" *tatione juris cenfetur eadem perfona nobifcum, digno*
" *præveniamus honore et fæcundâ gratiâ perfequamur.*"

invest

inveſt them with the natural rights of an animal *.

But though I am willing to ſuppoſe them rather thus criminally deceitful in this ſham law, than load them with a more heinous imputation ; I do not mean to juſtify ſuch fallacy. Were it poſſible, which I am ſincerely very far from admitting, that any Engliſh ſovereign could demand from his miniſters the unnatural power contained in this act; it would

---

* It muſt be remembered by the reader, that marriage is the only *legal* intercourſe between the ſexes. And that the right of marriage is the moſt eſſential natural right of mankind, may be inconteſtably concluded from this obſervation, in which all naturaliſts concur ; viz. That nature has been much more ſolicitous for the procreation than the preſervation of animals. Be it alſo remembered that no man can have a right to that, from which another man has at the ſame time a right to debar him.

have

have been their duty to repeat to him the old English fable of Canute and his flatterers; and to remind him, that the God of nature has graciously provided that this torrent can no more be repelled than the ocean.

But, whether deceiving or deceived, I am firmly perfuaded that the fault of this act of parliament, of this sham law (which will for ever be a reproach to the parliament which could enact it *) is chiefly their

---

* By this act (if it could be a law) a king of England would be impowered to defeat the regular fucceffion (a matter of the laft importance to the happiness of every country), and to determine in which branch of the family the Royalty should defcend: for he might refuse his confent to the elder and grant it to the younger. Had his late majefty king George the fecond been in poffeffion of this power, and capable of applying

their own. It has been faid (but I believe not truly) that men are born poets:
and I have read (what is ftill more extraordinary) that the Houfe of Auftria has
the power of *making* poets. Be it fo. But
no man is born a lawyer; and no fovereign
is able to make one. His majefty, I am
confident, required no more from his minifters than fuch proper and prudent and
legal regulations and reftraints as a father
might juftly and affectionately provide and
employ againft the poffible inconfideration

---

applying it, the pofterity of the late duke of Cumber-
land might have been at this day upon the throne; or
(what is a much more likely effect and confequence of
fuch unjuft laws) the contending iffue of two brothers,
claiming by different and difputed titles, might again
have deluged the land. Aye, But the Parliament—
Oh! yes. The Parliament! A parliament which could
pafs fuch a bill, would not ftartle at any application
of it.

and

and heedleſſneſs of youth. And it was their duty, in a reaſonable and becoming manner, (without injuſtice or degradation) to carry his royal and paternal deſigns into effectual and due execution. But they, either through ignorance or deſign, appearing by this act to have given him more power than he could wiſh or poſſibly obtain, have literally given him *none*. And their royal highneſſes may reſt aſſured that (ſolemnized as I underſtand their marriage to have been) the honourable union between them is, not only in conſcience but in law, as firm as formal and as ſolid, as any other civil contract that can poſſibly be effected between men : and is not in the leaſt impeached by this moſt wicked as well as moſt ridiculous act of parliament *.

---

* It is alſo to be obſerved, that the Royal family is excepted from the proviſions of the Marriage-Act, 26. Geo. II. chap. 33. § 17.

5   But

But the ferious part of this bufinefs, I am told, and that which gives a much more real and well-founded alarm, even for the fafety of *Church* and *State* *, is— That his royal highnefs has married a *Papift*. And an act of parliament, 1 W. and M. ft. 2. c. 2. § 9. enacts, that— " Whereas it hath been found by expe- " rience, that it is inconfiftent with the " fafety and welfare of this proteftant

---

* Report has attributed thefe words and this alarm to a gentleman whom the news-papers and certain witty gentlemen have long feemed determined to run down; whilft they afcribe to him the only open, ho- neft, manly and independent conduct on this occafion. But though their wit is fterling, he may fafely fet them at defiance. It is not words but conduct which finally decides a man's character. And he feems to have that about him which is better than talents and genius, and which at the long run will leave them both at a diftance behind.

" king-

" kingdom, to be governed by a popifh
" prince, or by any king or queen *marry-*
" *ing a papift* ; the faid lords fpiritual and
" temporal and commons do farther pray
" that it may be enacted, that all and
" every perfon and perfons that is, are,
" or fhall be reconciled to, or fhall hold
" communion with, the fee or church of
" Rome, or fhall profefs the popifh reli-
" gion, or *fhall marry a papift*, fhall be
" excluded and be for ever incapable to
" inherit, poffefs or enjoy the crown and
" government of this realm and Ireland,
" and the dominions thereunto belonging,
" or any part of the fame, or to have, ufe
" or exercife any regal power, authority
" or jurifdiction within the fame ; and in
" all and every fuch cafe or cafes the peo-
" ple of thefe realms fhall be, and are here-
" by abfolved of their allegiance ; and the
" faid crown and government fhall from
" time

" time to time defcend to and be enjoyed
" by fuch perfon or perfons, being pro-
" teftants, as fhould have inherited and
" enjoyed the fame in cafe the faid perfon
" or perfons fo reconciled to, holding
" communion, or profeffing, or *marrying*
" as aforefaid, were naturally dead."

The above act of William and Mary is alfo confirmed by another act of parliament, 12 and 13 W. III. c. 2. By which the crown of thefe realms was fettled on the Houfe of Hanover.

Thefe acts of parliament I acknowledge to be laws; and moft facred laws indeed. They violate no rights. They who made them knew fomething more of their profeffion than they who framed the ridiculous act 12 Geo. III.

D   To

To govern a nation is no man's natural right : and a whole people are well authorized (for it is *their* natural right) to fix and determine upon what conditions they will accept a fovereign. And here it is well worth the reader's while attentively to obferve and notice the different path which different perfons purfue, though both have the fame object in contemplation. Behold one of the ftrongeft contrafts in legiflation between the meafures purfued by rafh ignorance and want of principle, and thofe adopted by cautious wifdom and ftrict regard to juftice. The object of the German legiflators was to keep the fucceffion pure and unmixed in the fovereign families. The object of the act of exclufion and the act of fettlement was to bar the iffue of a papift. A modern Englifh law-monger would have found the remedy to be one of the eafieft

I

and

and ſhorteſt things in the world. The
rights of all mankind would not have coſt
him a moment. He unties nothing, but
cuts through all. He would have paſſed
a bill at once to make all contravening
marriages impoſſible.—Not ſo our wiſer
anceſtors *. They left all men in the full
poſſeſſion of their natural rights; and obtained their honeſt end by exerting their
own. They attempted not to make any
man's marriage impoſſible; but ſettled

---

* " Qu'il me ſoit permis de le dire ici en paſſant,
" quelle difference entre de tels hommes et ceux qui,
" abuſant du droit de legiſlation, ont etabli des loix
" qui, même après que le genre humain a été delivré
" d'eux, perpétuent encore les malheurs du monde
" pendant la ſuite des ſiecles." Voyages d'un philo-
ſophe, p. 77. I quote from this book of Monſ. Poivre
merely for the pleaſure of naming him; becauſe he
ought to be read and remembered by every honeſt
man.

fairly

fairly the provifos and conditions of government.

Thefe acts.of parliament then I acknowledge to have the full force of law. But
they affect the fucceffion, not the marriage.
And if they were applicable and applied in
the prefent inftance, I confefs I fhould ·
confider it as a very ferious and fubftantial
mifchief to the country. But before I
enter upon their application, I defire to
fay a few words upon the act of fettlement. The provifions of that act were
wife and falutary. Some of them however were efpecially adapted to the peculiar
circumftances of the time : though fome
were fit to be of everlafting obligation.
Amongft the former I reckon, the prohibition to the fovereign of " going out of
" the dominions of England, Scotland, or
" Ireland."

" Ireland *." And the exclufion of thofe who were or fhould be married to a papift. The firft of thefe was repealed at the very firft moment when it could poffibly take any effect, viz. in the firft year of George the firft, for whofe acceffion alone this prohibition was efpecially calculated. And if the *fecond* were now, by a fimilar but much more reafonable complaifance, re-pealed (with the exception only of papift *fovereign* families; which would ftill fecure the object intended) I own it would meet with my moft hearty concurrence.

Amongft the *latter* I reckon the two following conditions, which were bafely,

---

* " That no perfon who fhall hereafter come to " the poffeffion of this crown, fhall go out of the " dominions of England, Scotland, or Ireland, with- " out confent of parliament."

and

and for as bafe a purpofe, furrendered to queen Anne, and repealed within five years after they had been enacted, viz.

" That from and after the time that
" the farther limitation by this act fhall
" take effect, all matters and things re-
" lating to the well-governing of this
" kingdom, which are properly cogniza-
" ble in the Privy Council by the laws ·
" and cuftoms of this realm, *fhall be*
" *tranfacted there*, and all refolutions
" taken thereupon *fhall be figned* by fuch
" of the Privy Council as fhall advife and
" confent to the fame."

And " That no perfon who has an of-·
" fice or place of profit under the king,
" or receives a penfion from the crown,
" fhall be capable of ferving as a member
" of the houfe of commons."

Now

Now though it may not be reckoned a very handfome proceeding at any time to bargain with a fovereign; I own myfelf fo much of a chapman, that I fhould be ftrongly inclined to feize the opportunity, whenever it offered, for re-enacting thefe two wholefome conditions : and fhould be more than willing, even anxious, to barter the papift marriage for the refponfibility of counfellors, and the independence of the reprefentative body; being much more eafily contented to truft the fovereign with a papift wife, than with a corrupt parliament. But fome confciences, I know, will ftill be ftraining at a gnat, and popery is now become no more; whilft they gulp down greedily the camel of corruption, which is now become a monfter.

But whatever may be my opinion or wifhes on the fubject, and however rea-

fonable

fonable the repeal of this condition may at this time appear to others as well as to myfelf; it is not to be denied that it ſtands at preſent in full force, and is the undoubted law of the land. There let it ſtand, a ſcarecrow for the ſpiritleſs. But however the letter of the law may abſolve, I do not believe that Engliſhmen ever did or ever will renounce their allegiance to an honeſt and juſt prince, merely on account of the religious opinions or fancies of his conſort. Againſt an unjuſt, an uſurping, or undermining prince, every plauſible pretence of the ſubjeċt to caſt him off would be juſtifiable: and on ſuch occaſions indeed, where juſtice and liberty have been the real and fundamental cauſes of the quarrel, it has often happened, as Oliver Cromwell very fairly told his fanatical hypocrites, that " God has thrown
" religion

" religion as a make-weight into 'the
" fcale *."

But I may fpare myfelf the trouble of
reafoning on this queftion, or of fhewing,
as may eafily be fhewn, the ready means
of evading this law; fince it admits a
more direct reply. This law will not be

---

* The commiffioners who were fent by the parliament during the war to treat with the king at Oxford for peace, were of the fame opinion: for Lord
Clarendon tells us, that—" In all matters which re-
" lated to the *church*, they did not only defpair of the
" king's concurrence, but *did not* in their own judg-
" ments *wifh it*; and believed that the *ftrength of the*
" *party* which defired the continuance of the war,
" was made up of thofe who were *very indifferent*
" *in that point*; and that, if they might return
" *with fatisfaction in other particulars*, they fhould
" have power enough in the two houfes to oblige the
" more violent people to accept or fubmit to the con-
" ditions."

applied,

applied, for it is not applicable, to the prefent cafe. Whatever religious opinions *Mrs. Fitzherbert* may or may not have formerly entertained (a matter perfectly indifferent) *her royal highnefs* is NOT a papift. And whoever fhall affert the contrary, if they mean to do it either with honefty or fafety to themfelves, fhould take good care to be well provided with evidence.

I think I am well juftified in afferting, that fince the period of her marriage, her royal highnefs has not performed any one act of any kind whatever, which can juftify fuch a denomination. And not only my own opinion of her underftanding and good fenfe affures me of it, but fuch authority as leaves no doubt in my mind confirms the affurance, that fhe is both ready and willing at any time to give proof.

of

of her conformity to the eſtabliſhed religion of the land.

I conclude therefore (and truſt that
others will conclude with me) that his
royal highneſs's marriage is neither *un-*
uſual, nor *improper,* nor *impoſſible,* nor *il-*
legal, nor affected by the act of *excluſion*
or the act of *ſettlement* ; but ſuch as does
honour to his ſentiments, and is highly
beneficial to his country.

POST-

POSTSCRIPT.

May, 1787.

SINCE the conclufion of my Letter, I have been informed upon Newf-paper authority, that the marriage in quef-tion has been formally and folemnly dif-avowed; the very fuppofition reprefent-ed as abfurd and ridiculous; and the re-port of it, as originating in wilful flander and malice !

If this pretended difavowal were well founded, I confefs I fhould be much mor-tified: for I had a fingular fatisfaction in beholding this act of parliament, *the firft of its kind*, inftantly violated (as it ought to be) by the perfon whom it could firft affect, the eldeft of the king's family. It

is

is not confined to any one kingdom, but for the benefit of mankind at large, that in all countries the violation of all such acts of power without principle, fhould follow as clofely as poffible upon the heels of their promulgation. There is no other effectual method of forcing inftruction upon ignorant, though perhaps not ill-meaning, legiflators.

But I am determined not to believe this Newfpaper authority. On the contrary, I confider this ftory of a difavowal to be itfelf an additional flander on a much mifunderftood and mifreprefented young man. I have no doubt (for he is young and a prince) that fome things, though I know them not, might poffibly be changed for the better in his conduct. But I will not believe, that at any time, and leaft of all in the moment and man-

ner

ner as reported, fuch a difvowal (be the marriage true or falfe), or any thing tending to leffen the character of the lady, could poffibly be authorized by him. And, though extremely difgufted with his politics, yet I have too much perfonal refpect for Mr. Fox, to believe, upon the authority of a newfpaper, that Mr. Fox was either the advifer, or filent feeming approver, much lefs the medium of fuch a difavowal. If fuch a meafure had been thought advifable, or even neceffary, upon any important fcore; yet Mr. Fox knows better how to time even his neceffary meafures. What! at the moment when the payment of debts and revenue were the queftions, then to get up and make this difavowal; and thus give it the appearance of facrificing, on compulfion, a defencelefs woman's character (with whom I fuppofe, at leaft there was friendfhip)
for

for fo mean a confideration as a paltry fum of money ! No. I will never believe it. Becaufe I remember very well what a half-civilized barbarian replied to his un-civilized counfellors, who advifed him to give up a MAN, not a WOMAN, to the *extreme neceffity* of his fituation ;—" No, " replied the prince: I can refign my " dominions even up to the walls of my " metropolis ; for in happier circum- " ftances they may hereafter be recovered: " but the forfeiture of honour in a fove- " reign can never be retrieved." Here we fee, that with fuch unprincipled coun-fellors as thefe, had this magnanimous prince been younger or more diffident, the example of an illuftrious character * would probably have been loft to the world.

---

* Peter the Great, Czar of Ruffia.

And

And that I do not exaggerate the confequence of fuch a difavcwal, is evident
from the confequence even of the report.
For on the Tuefday following, May 1,
this is the rational comment of the *Courier
de l'Europe.*

" La fable du pretendu mariage de S.
" A. R. *Mgr*. le prince de Galles a enfin
" été expliquée en plein parlement de
" maniere à ne plus laiffer de doute.
" C'eft une explication qui eft d'autant
" plus facheufe pour *Mme. F—b—t,* que
" l'on a fuppofé des liens entre S. A. R.
" et cette dame, fur lefquels on n'avoit
" pas encore prononcé. Jufqu'ici *Mme.*
" *F—b—t* a été recue dans toutes les
" focietés où étoit invité le prince; *mais*
" *il ne fera guére poffible aujourdhui qu'elle*
" *jouiffe des mêmes avantages,* à moins que
" cette premiére explication n'en entraine
" une

" une autre, et que la prétendue inti-
" mité de S. A. R. ne foit prefentée fous
" des couleurs *admiffibles en bonne com-*
" *pagnie.*"

Such is the cruel but natural conclufion,
to the prejudice of a character in the moft
defencelefs fituation upon earth : for the
fame fenfe of honour which, operating
upon others, fhould have prevented the
occafion; operating upon her, reftrains
her even from her own juftification.

But though I will not, for thefe reafons, believe the report, as far as it relates
to his royal highnefs, or to Mr. Fox ; and
cannot but ridicule the fuggefted juftification, of an ill-timed complaifance to certain fcrupulous country gentlemen of the
party ; yet I can eafily fuppofe, that there
might not be wanting fome falfe friends

E   about

about his royal highnefs, in order to ingratiate themfelves, or at leaft to avoid the hazard of offending *elfewhere*, ready enough and willing to advife fo degrading a ftep *.

And

* What thofe about a court are capable of, on fuch occafions, may be collected from the treatment which the mother of our two laft queens, Mary and Anne, met with in her day, when fhe was in a fimilar fituation.

" Le mariage du Duc d'Yorck avec la fille du Chancelier, n'avoit manqué d'aucune des circonftances, qui rendent les unions de cette nature valides à l'égard du ciel. L'intention de part et d'autre, la cérémonie dans les formes, les témoins, et le point effentiel du facrement en avoient été. Le Duc dans les premiéres douceurs de ce mariage, loin de s'en repentir, fembloit ne fouhaiter le rétabliffement du roi que pour le déclarer avec éclat ; mais dés que la poffeffion de Mademoifelle Hyde n'avoit plus de charmes nouveaux pour lui, il envifageoit fon mariage comme un attentat contre le refpect et l'obéiffance qu'il devoit au roi. D'un autre côté fe prefentoient les larmes et

le

And it would not be wonderful if no real
friend were found, in such a conjuncture,
to

---

le défefpoir de la pauvre Hyde : et plus que cela les
remords de confcience. Au milieu de ces differentes
agitations il s'ouvrit à Milord Falmouth, et le confulta
fur le parti qu'il devoit prendre. Falmouth lui foûtint
d'abord, non feulement qu'il n'étoit pas marié, mais
qu'il ètoit impoffible qu'il y eût jamais fongé ; qu' un
mariage ètoit nul pour lui fans le confentement du roi.
Que c'étoit une mocquerie de mettre en jeu la fille
d'un petit avocat : qu'à l'égard de fes fcrupules, il
n'avoit qu'à vouloir bien écouter des gens qui l'in-
ftruiroient à fond de la conduite que Mademoifelle
Hyde avoit tenue avant qu'il la connût ; et que pourvû
qu'il ne leur dit point que la chofe fût déja faite, il
auroit bientôt de quoi le déterminer. Le Duc d'Yorck
confentit, et Milord Falmouth aiant affemblé fon con-
feil et fes témoins, les mena dans le cabinet de fon
Alteffe, après les avoir inftruits de ce qu'on leur vou-
loit. Ces meffieurs étoient le Comte d'Arran, Germain, Talbot et Killegrew, tous *gens d'honneur.* Le
Duc leur aiant dit, que quoiqu' ils n'ignoraffent pas fa
tendreffe pour Mademoifelle Hyde, ils pouvoient ig-

to encourage and fortify his royal highnefs in the refolution of his own manly
mind :

---

norer à quels engagements cette tendreffe l'avoit porté,
qu'il fe croioit obligé de tenir toutes les paroles qu'il
avoit pû lui donner; mais comme de certains bruits,
faux ou veritables, s'étoient repandus au fujet de fa
conduite, il les prioit comme amis, et leur ordonnoit
par tout ce qu'ils lui devoient, de lui dire fincerement
ce qu'ils en fçavoient, d'autant qu'il étoit réfolu
de régler fur leur temoignages les deffeins qu'il
avoit pour elle. On fe fit un peu tirer l'oreille
d'abord, et l'on fit femblant de n'ofer prononcer
fur une matiére fi férieufe et fi délicate; mais le Duc
d'Yorck ayant réiteré fes inftances, chacun fe mit à
déduire par le menu ce qu'il fçavoit, et peut-être ce
qu'il ne fçavoit pas, de la pauvre Hyde. On y joignit
toutes les circonftances qu'il falloit, pour appuier le té-
moignage. Par exemple, le Comte d'Arran, qui parla
le premier, depofa, que dans la gallerie de Hons-laer-
dyk, où la Comteffe d'Offery, fa belle-fœur, et Germain jouoient un jour aux quilles, Mademoifelle avoit
fait femblant de fe trouver mal, et s'étoit rétirée dans
une chambre au bout de la gallerie; que lui dépofant
l'avoit

mind : for though all princes have pro-
feſſing friends numerous enough to their
face,

---

l'avoit ſuivie, et que lui aiant coupé ſon lacet pour
donner plus de vraiſemblance aux vapeurs, il avoit fait
de ſon mieux pour la ſecourir, ou pour la défennuier.
Talbot dit qu'elle lui avoit donné un rendezvous dans
le cabinet du chancelier, tandis, qu'il étoit au conſeil,
à telles enſeignes, que n'ayant pas tant d'attention aux
choſes qui étoient ſur la table, qu'à celle qui les occu-
poit alors, ils avoient fait repandre toute l'encre d'une
bouteille, ſur une dépéche de quatre pages, et que le
ſinge du roi qu'on accuſoit de ce déſordre, en avoit
été long-tems en diſgrace. Germain indiqua pluſieurs
endroits où il avoit en des audiences longues et favour-
ables. Cependant tous ces chefs d'accuſation ne rou-
loient que ſur quelques tendres privautés, ou tout au
plus, ſur ce qu'on appelle les menus plaiſirs d'un com-
merce ; mais Killegrew voulant rencherir ſur ces foibles
dépoſitions, dit tout net, qu'il avoit eu l'honneur de
ſes bonnes graces. Il aſſura qu'il avoit trouvé l'heure
du Berger dans un certain cabinet conſtruit au-deſſus
de l'eau, à toute autre fin que d'étre favorable aux em-
preſſemens amoureux ; qu'il avoit eu pour témoins de

ſon

face, yet had they no more coats than real friends to their back, I am afraid moſt ſovereigns would go naked.

And

ſon bonheur trois ou quatre cignes, qui pouvoient bien avoir été témoins du bonheur de bien d'autres dans ce même cabinet, vû qu'elle y alloit ſouvent, et qu'elle s'y plaiſoit fort. Le Duc d'York trouva cette derniére accuſation outrée, perſuadé qu'il avoit par devers lui des preuves ſuffiſantes du contraire. Il remercia Meſſieurs les témoins à bonne fortune de leur franchiſe, leur impoſa ſilence à l'avenir ſur ce qu'ils venoient de lui déclarer, et paſſa dans l'appartement du roi. Le Duc d'Yorck, en ſortant, parut tellement émû, qu'ils ne douterent point que tout n'allât mal pour la pauvre Hyde. Milord Falmouth commençoit à s'attendrir de ſa diſgrace, et ſe repentoit *un peu* de la part qu'il y avoit eue, lorſque le Duc d'Yorck lui dit de ſe trouver avec le comte d'Oſſery chez le chancelier dans une heure. Ils furent un peu ſurpris qu'il eût la dureté d'annoncer lui-même cette accablante nouvelle. Ils trouverent à l'heure marquée Son Alteſſe dans la chambre de mademoiſelle Hyde. Ses yeux paroiſſoient mouillés de quelques larmes,

And I can the more eaſily believe this, becauſe it is notorious that ſome ſuch muſt have

---

larmes, qu'elle s'efforçoit de retenir. Le Chancelier appuyé contre la muraille, leur parut bouffi de quelque choſe. Ils ne doutérent point que ce ne fût de rage et de deſeſpoir. Le Duc d'Yorck leur dit de cet air content et ſerain dont on annonce les bonnes nouvelles, " comme vous êtes les deux hommes de la cour que " j'eſtime le plus, je veux que vous aiez les premiers " l'honneur de ſaluer la ducheſſe d'Yorck : La voilà." La ſurpriſe ne ſervoit de rien, et l'étonnement n'étoit pas de ſaiſon dans cette conjonĉture. Ils en étoient pourtant ſi remplis, que pour s'en cacher ils ſe jettérent promptement à genoux pour lui baiſer la main, qu'elle leur tendit avec autant de grandeur et de majeſté, que ſi de ſa vie elle n'eût fait autre choſe. Le lendemain la nouvelle en fut publique, et toute la cour s'empreſſa par devoir à lui témoigner des reſpeĉts, *qui devinrent très-ſinceres dans la ſuite.* Les petits-maitres qui avoient dépoſé contre elle à toute autre intention que ce qu'ils voyoient, ſe trouvérent fort deconcertés. Les femmes ne ſont pas trop d'humeur à pardonner de certaines injures, et quand elles ſe promettent le plaiſir de la

vengeance,

have been about him, when he was missed
to an *arrangement* which no doubt was

repre-

---

vengeance, elles n'y vont pas de main-morte : cependant ils n'en eurent que la peur. La Duchesse d'Yorck
instruite de tout ce qui s'étoit dit dans le cabinet sur
son chapitre, loin d'en temoigner du ressentiment, af-
fecta de distinguer par toutes sortes de gracieusetés et
de bons offices ceux qui l'avoient attaquée par des en-
droit si sensibles. Jamais elle ne leur en parla que pour
louer leur zéle, et pour leur dire, que rien ne mar-
quoit plus le dévouement d'un honnête homme, que de
prendre un peu sur sa probité, pour donner aux intérêts
d'un maitre, ou d'un ami. Rare exemple de prudence
et de moderation, non-seulement pour le sexe, mais
pour ceux qui se parent le plus de philosophie dans le
nôtre." Memoires du Comte de Grammont, p. 186.

In the second volume of the *Continuation of the Life
of Edward Earl of Clarendon (written by himself)* we
have also some account of the same transaction. In
which the haughty and furious conduct of the Queen
Dowager, a daughter of France, and whose passions,
prejudices and counsels had before greatly contributed

to

reprefented to him, as it has been puffed
to the public, as a conduct highly honourable;

to all the mifchiefs which befel her hufband Charles the
Firft; the meannefs and hypocrify of the over-acted
part of Mr. Hyde, the Chancellor, who manifefted
none of that " *dignity of fentiment*" prepofteroufly attributed to him by his Oxford Editor; the bafenefs, un-
fteadinefs, and want of principle of the Duke of York,
and of his tools the Courtiers; are well contrafted with
the calm and patient propriety of Mifs Hyde's conduct;
the gentlemanlike and temperate behaviour of the
King; and the wife indifference of the Public.

" The firft matter of general and public importance
" was the difcovery of a great affection that the Duke
" had for the Chancellor's daughter, and of a contract
" of marriage between them. The Duke's affection
" and kindnefs had been much fpoken of beyond the
" feas, but without the leaft fufpicion in any body that
" it could ever tend to marriage. But now upon this
" difcovery, the Chancellor (Mr. Hyde) looked upon
" himfelf as a ruined perfon, and that the king's in-
" dignation would fall upon him as the contriver.
" And the leaft calamity that he expected upon himfelf
" and

able ; but which he will ſtart from with
indignation whenever he conſiders it properly.

" and family was to end his days in poverty and miſery.
" —The Duke informed the King of the affeĉtion and
" engagement that had been long between him and
" Miſs Hyde, that they had been long contraĉted, and
" that ſhe was with child ; and therefore with all
" imaginable importunity he begged his majeſty's
" leave and permiſſion upon his knees, that he might
" publicly marry her, in ſuch a manner as his majeſty
" thought neceſſary for the conſequence thereof ; and
" his paſſion was expreſſed in a very wonderful man-
" ner, and with many tears, proteſting, that if his ma-
" jeſty ſhould not give his conſent, he would imme-
" diately leave the kingdom, and muſt ſpend his life in
. " foreign parts. His majeſty preſently ſent for the
" Marquis of Ormond and the Earl of Southampton,
" who he well knew were Mr. Hyde's boſom-friends,
. " and informed them at large, and of all particulars
" which had paſſed from the Duke to him, and com-
" manded them preſently to ſee for the Chancellor to
" come to his own chamber at Whitehall, where they
" would meet him upon a buſineſs of great importance,
" which

perly. What will be his feelings hereafter, if fome Ambaffador of his own,
fhall

" which the King had commended to them for their
" joint advice. They no fooner met, than the Mar-
" quis of Ormond told the Chancellor, that he had a
" matter to inform him of, that he doubted would give
" him much trouble; and therefore advifed him to
" compofe himfe'. to hear it: and then told him, that
" the Duke of York had owned a great affection for
" his daughter to the King, and that he much doubted
" that fhe was with child by the Duke, and that the
" King required the advice of them and of him, what
" he was to do. The Chancellor broke out into a
" very immoderate paffion againft the *wickednefs* of his
" daughter; and faid with all imaginable earneftnefs,
" that as foon as he came home, he would *turn her*
" *out of his houfe*, as a ftrumpet, *to fhift for her-*
" *felf*, and would never fee her again. They told
" him, that his paffion was too violent to admi-
" nifter good counfel to him, that they thought
" that the Duke was married to his daughter, and
" that there were other meafures to be taken, than
" thofe which the diforder he was in had fuggefted to
" him.

fhall in a foreign land retire from the fta-
tion and dignity which he was appointed

to

" him. Whereupon he fell into new commotions,
" and faid, if that were true, he was well prepared to
" advife what was to be done : that *he had much rather*
" *his daughter fhould be the duke's whore than his wife.*
" But if there were any reafon to fufpect the other, he
" was ready to give a pofitive judgment, in which he
" hoped their lordfhips would concur with him; that
" the king fhould immediately caufe the woman [*N. B.*
" *the pregnant wife of the prefumptive heir to the crown*]
" to be fent to the Tower, and to be caft into a *dungeon,*
" under fo ftrict a guard that no perfon living fhould
" be admitted to come to her; and then that an act
" of parliament fhould be immediately paffed for the
" —*cutting off her head*; to which he would not only
" give his confent, but would very willingly be the firft
" man that fhould propofe it. In this point of time
" the king entered the room and fate down at the
" table ; and perceiving by his countenance the *agony*
" the chancellor was in, and his *fwollen eyes* from
" whence a *flood of tears* had fallen, he afked the other
" lords what they had done, and whether they had re-
" folved

to uphold as the reprefentative of his fovereign, in order to apply the income of

his

" folved on any thing. The Earl of Southampton
" faid, his majefty muft confult with foberer men;
" that he (pointing to the chancellor) was mad, and
" had propofed fuch extravagant things, that he was
" no more to be confulted with. Whereupon his
" majefty, looking upon him with a wonderful be-
" nignity, faid, Chancellor, I knew this bufinefs would
" trouble you ; and therefore I appointed your two
" friends to confer firft with you upon it, before I
" would fpeak with you myfelf; but you muft now
" lay afide all paffion that difturbs you, and confider
" that this bufinefs will not do itfelf ; that it will
" quickly take air ; and therefore it is fit that I firft
" refolve what to do, before other men uncalled pre-
" fume to give the counfel ; tell me therefore what
" you would have me do, and I will follow your ad-
" vice. Then his majefty enlarged upon the paffion
" of his brother, and the expreffions he had often ufed,
" that he was not capable of having any other wife,
" and the like. Upon which the chancellor arofe,
" and with a little compofednefs faid, Sir, I hope I
" need

his office to the difcharge of his debts ;
and thus attempt to avoid the reproach òf
private

―――――――――――――

" need make no apology to you for myfelf and of my
" own in this matter, upon which I look with fo
" much deteftation, that though I could have wifhed
" that your brother had not thought it fit to have put
" this difgrace upon me, I had much rather fubmit
" and bear it with all humility, than that it fhould be
" repaired by making her his wife ; the thought where-
" of I do fo much abominate, that I had much rather
" fee her dead, with all the infamy that is due to her
" prefumption. And then he repeated all that he had
" before faid to the lords, of fending her prefently to
" the Tower, and the reft ; and concluded,—Sir, I
" do *upon all my oaths which I have taken to you* to give
" you faithful counfels, and from all the fincere gra-
" titude I ftand obliged to you for fo many obligations,
" renew this counfel to you ; and do befeech you to
" purfue it, as the only expedient that can free you
" from the *evils that this bufinefs will otherwife bring*
" *upon you.*—But he obferved by the king's counte-
" nance that he was not pleafed with his advice. This
" fubject was quickly the matter of all men's dif-
" courfe,

private infolvency, by the mifapplication of public money ? The revenue of the Prince

---

" courfe, and *did not produce thofe murmurs and dif-*
" *contented reflections* which were expected. The par-
" liament was fitting, and took *not the leaft notice of*
" *it ; nor could it be difcerned that many were fcandalized*
" *at it.* The king fpake every day about it, and told
" the chancellor, that he muft behave himfelf wifely,
" for that the thing was remedilefs ; and that his ma-
" jefty knew that they were married, which would
" quickly appear to all men, who knew that nothing
" could be done upon it. In this time the chancellor
" had conferred with his daughter, and not only dif-
" covered that they were unqueftionably married, but
" by whom, and who were prefent at it, who would
" be ready to avow it. And he faw *no other remedy*
" *could be applied, but that which he had propofed to the*
" *king,* who thought of nothing like it. When the
" Princefs royal came to town, there grew to be a great
" filence in that affair. The Duke faid nothing to the
" chancellor, nor came nor fent to his daughter as he
" had conftantly ufed to do : and it was induftrioufly
" publifhed about the town, that that bufinefs was
" broken

Prince of Wales is granted to the Heir
Apparent to live like the Heir Apparent;
and

" broken off, and that the duke was refolved never to
" think more of it. The Queen had before written a
" very fharp letter to the duke, full of indignation,
" that he fhould have fo low thoughts as to marry fuch
" a woman. And now fhe fent the king word, that
" fhe was on the way to England, to prevent with her
" authority fo great a ftain and difhonour to the crown;
" and ufed many threats and paffionate expreffions up-
" on the fubject. Rumours were fpread that the queen
" was coming with a purpofe to complain to the par-
" liament, and to apply the higheft remedies to pre-
" vent fo great a mifchief. In the mean time it was
" reported abroad, that the duke had difcovered fome
" difloyalty in the lady, which he had never fufpected,
" but had now fo full evidence of it, that he was re-
" folved never more to fee her; and that *He was not*
" *married*. And *all his family*, whereof the Lord Berk-
" ley and his nephew were the chief, fpake very loudly
" and fcandaloufly of it. The king carried himfelf
" with extraordinary grace towards the chancellor,
" and was with him more, and fpake upon all occa-
" fions

and *in truſt* that he will maintain a cor-
reſpondent ſtate : for his dignity is the
dignity

" ſions and before all perſons more gracȋouſly of him
" than ever. He told him with much trouble that his
" brother was abuſed ; and that there was a wicked
" conſpiracy ſet on foot by villains, which in the end,
" muſt prove of more diſhonour to the duke, than to
" any body elſe. The queen was now ready to em-
" bark, enflamed and haſtened by this occaſion ; and
" it was fit for the king and the duke, to wait on her
" at the ſhore. The queen expreſſed her indignation
" to the king and duke, with her natural paſſion,
" from the time of her meeting ; and the duke aſked
" her pardon for having placed his affection ſo un-
" equally, of which he was ſure there was now an end ;
" and that *He was not married*; and had now ſuch
" evidence of her unworthineſs, that he ſhould no
" more think of her. And it was now avowedly ſaid,
" that Sir Charles Berkley, *who was captain of his*
" *guard*, and in much more credit and favour with
" the duke than his uncle (though a young man of a
" diſſolute life and prone to all wickedneſs in the judg-
" ment of all ſober men) had informed the duke, that

F   " he

dignity of the nation, and the revenue is not his to apply to any other purpofe.

An

" he was bound in confcience to preferve him from
" taking to wife a woman fo wholly unwcrthy of him ;
" that he himfelf had lain with her ; and that for his
" fake he would be content to marry her, though he
" knew well the familiarity the duke had had with her.
" This evidence with fo folemn oaths prefented by a
" perfon fo much loved and trufted by him, made a
" wonderful impreffion in the duke ; and now con-
" firmed by the commands of his mother, as he had
" been before prevailed upon by his fifter, *He refolved*
" *to deny that he was married:* and never to fee the
" woman again, who had been fo falfe to him.   And
" the Queen being fatisfied with this refolution, they
" came all to London with a full hope that they fhould
" prevail, to the utter overthrow of the Chancellor ;
" the King having, without any reply or debate, heard
" all they faid of the other affair, and his mother's bit-
" ternefs againft him.   The king continued his grace
" towards the chancellor without the leaft diminution ;
" which made it evident that he believed nothing of
" what Sir Charles Berkley avowed, and looked on

" him

An oppofition without any one *public* principle, either real or even *profeſſed*, might
naturally

" him as a fellow of great wickednefs. In the mean
" time the feafon of his daughter's delivery was at
" hand. And it was the king's *chance* to be at his
" houfe with the committee of Council, when fhe fell
" in labour : of which being advertifed by her father,
" the king directed him to fend for the Lady Marchio-
" nefs of Ormond, the Countefs of Sunderland, and
" other ladies of known honour and fidelity to the
" crown, to be prefent with her. Who all came, and
" were prefent till fhe was delivered of a fon. The
" bifhop of Winchefter, in the interval of her greateft
" pangs, and fometimes when they were upon her, was
" prefent, and afked her fuch queftions as were thought
" fit for the occafion.—Whofe the child was of which
" fhe was in labour ? Whom fhe averred with all pro-
" teftations to be the Duke's. Whether fhe had ever
" known any other man ? Which fhe renounced
" with all vehemence, faying, that fhe was confi-
" dent the Duke did not think fhe had. And being
" afked, Whether fhe were married to the Duke ?
" She anfwered, She was; and that there were wit-

" neffes

naturally conclude their adverfaries to have
as little principle as themfelves ; and feek
a ground

" nefles enough, who in due time fhe was confident
" would avow it. In a word, her behaviour was
" fuch as abundantly fatisfied the ladies who were pre-
" fent, of her innocence from the reproach ; and they
" were not referved in the declaration of it, even be-
" fore the perfons who were the leaft pleafed with
" their teftimony. And the lady marchionefs of Or-
" mond took an opportunity to declare it fully to the
" Duke himfelf, and perceived in him fuch a kind of
" tendernefs, that perfuaded her that he did not be-
" lieve any thing amifs. And the king enough pub-
" lifhed his opinion and judgment of the fcandal. The
" Duke however told the Chancellor, that for his
" daughter, fhe had behaved herfelf fo foully (of which
" he had fuch evidence as was as convincing as his
" own eyes, and of which he could make no doubt)
" that nobody could blame him for his behaviour to-
" wards her. The chancellor replied, that *he was not*
" *concerned to vindicate his daughter from any the moft*
" *improbable fcandals and afperfions.* He would leave
" that to God Almighty, upon whofe blefling he would
" depend,

a ground for minifterial odium and popular complaint even in their own difhonour-

able

" depend, whilft himfelf remained innocent, and no
" longer. There did *not* after all this *appear in the*
" *difcourfes of men, any of that humcur and indignaticn*
" *which was expected.* On the contrary, men of the
" greateft name and reputation fpake of the foulnefs
" of the proceeding with great freedom, and with all
" the deteftation imaginable againft Sir Charles Berk-
" ley, whofe teftimony nobody believed: not without
" fome cenfure of the chancellor, for not enough ap-
" pearing and profecuting the indignity. The queen's
" implacable difpleafure continued in the full height,
" doing all ʰe could to keep the duke firm to his re-
" folution, and to give all countenance to the calumny.
" At this time it pleafed God to vifit the Princefs Royal
" with the fmall pox, of which fhe died within few
" days; having in her laft agonies expreffed a diflike
" of the proceedings in that affair, to which fhe had
" contributed too much. The duke himfelf grew
" melancholick and difpirited, and cared not for com-
" pany, nor thofe divertifements in which he formerly
" delighted: which was obferved by every body, and

" which

able counfel and bad actions. What was
the complaint and the ground of application

" which in the end wrought fo far upon the confcience
" of the lewd informer, that he, Sir Charles Berkley,
" came to the duke, and clearly declared to him, that
" the general difcourfe of men, of what inconveni-
" ence and mifchief, if not abfolute ruin, fuch a mar-
" riage would be to his royal highnefs, had prevailed
" with him to ufe all the power he had to diffuade him
" from it: and when he found he could not prevail
" with him, he had formed that accufation, which he
" prefumed could not but produce the effect he wifh-
" ed; which he now confeffed to be falfe, and without
" the leaft ground; and that he was very confident of
" her virtue. And therefore befought his highnefs to
" pardon a fault that was committed out of pure de-
" votion to him, and that he would not fuffer him
" to be ruined by the power of thofe whom he had
" fo unworthily provoked; and of which he had fo
" much fhame, that he had not confidence to look
" upon them. The duke found himfelf fo much re-
" lieved in that part that moft afflicted him, that he
" *embraced him*, and made a folemn promife, that he
" *fhould*

tion to Parliament ? " It is a difgrace,
" fay they, to the nation, to fee the heir
" apparent

" *fhould not fuffer in the leaft degree in his own affection,*
" for what had proceeded fo abfolutely from his good-
" will to him ; and that he would take fo much care
" of him, that in the compounding that affair he
" fhould be fo comprehended, that he fhould receive
" no difadvantage. And now the duke appeared with
" another countenance, writ to her whom he had in-
" jured, that he would fpeedily vifit her ; and gave
" her charge, to have a care of his fon : and gave the
" king a full account of all, without concealing his
" joy. The queen was not pleafed with this change ;
" though the duke did not yet own to her that he had
" altered his refolution. She was always very angry
" at the king's coldnefs, who had been fo far from that
" averfion which fhe expected, that he found excufes for
" the duke, and endeavoured to divert her paffions ; and
" now preffed the difcovery of the truth by Sir Charles
" Berkley's confeffion, as a thing that pleafed him,
" But the queen having come to know that the duke
" had made a vifit at the place fhe moft abhorred, fhe
" brake into great paffion, and publicly declared, that

F 4 " when-

" apparent reduced to the ftyle and con-
" dition of a private gentleman !"—And
so

" whenever that woman fhould be brought into
" Whitehall by one door, her majefty would go
" out of it by another door, and never come into it
" again. And for feveral days her majefty would
" not fuffer the duke to come into her prefence.
" So that the duke's affair, which he now took to
" heart, was (as every body thought) to be left in the
" ftate it was, at leaft under the renunciation and in-
" terdiction of a mother. When on a fudden, of which
" nobody then knew the reafon, her majefty's coun-
" tenance and difcourfe was changed : fhe treated the
" duke with her ufual kindnefs, and confeffed to him,
" that the bufinefs that had offended her fo much, fhe
" perceived was proceeded fo far, that no remedy could
" be applied to it ; and therefore that fhe would trouble
" herfelf no farther in it, but pray to God to blefs him,
" and that he might be happy. So that the duke had
" now nothing to wifh, but that the queen would be
" reconciled to his wife, who remained ftill at her
" father's, where the king had vifited her often : to
" which the queen was not averfe, and fpake gracioufly
" of

ſo moſt undoubtedly it is. What more
ſevere condemnation then can be given, of
the

" of the chancellor, and ſaid ſhe would be good friends
" with him. The duke brought Sir Charles Berkley
" to the dutcheſs, at whoſe feet he caſt himſelf with
" all the acknowledgment and penitence he could ex-
" preſs ; and ſhe, according to the command of the
" duke, accepted his ſubmiſſion, and promiſed to for-
" get the offence. He came likewiſe to the chancel-
" lor with thoſe profeſſions which he could eaſily
" make ; and the other was obliged to receive him
" civilly. The king ſaid, there were many reaſons
" why he could never have deſigned nor adviſed his
" brother to this marriage ; yet ſince it was paſt, and
" all things ſo well reconciled, he would not deny
" that he was glad of it, and promiſed himſelf much
" benefit from it. He told the chancellor, that his
" daughter was a woman of great wit and excellent
" parts, and would have a great power with his bro-
" ther ; and that he knew that ſhe had an entire obe-
" dience for him, her father, who he knew would al-
" ways give her good counſel ; by which, he ſaid, he
" was confident that naughty people which had too
" much

the *counfel* and the *meafure* that thus dif-
graced the nation, than this which pro-
ceeds from their own lips? But they trufted (and, as it appears, with too good a
foundation) that minifters would not dare,
by an honeft performance of their duty
to the fovereign, to rifque the prince's
difpleafure by fpeaking the plain truth.
In my opinion I pay a much founder
compliment both to king and prince by

" much credit with his brother, and which had fo
" often mifled him, would be no more able to corrupt
" him: but that fhe would prevent all ill and unrea-
" fonable attempts: and therefore he again confeffed,
" that he was glad of it.——Thus an intrigue that
" without doubt had been entered into and induftri-
" oufly contrived by thofe who defigned to affront and
" bring-difhonour upon the chancellor and his family,
" was, by God's pleafure, turned to their fhame and
" reproach, and to the *increafe of the chancellor's*
" *greatnefs and profperity.*" [N. B. Yet he *fwore* that
he had rather have feen her *dead*, with all the *infamy*
due to her prefumption.]

believing,

believing, and shewing I believe, that the truth will not offend them. And, so trusting, I say that a clear, straight-forward conduct, without any by-regard, would have dictated this answer.———

" Both the manner and the matter of
" this application forbid acquiescence.
" The manner; because a government,
" that would be respected, must neither
" be bullied nor appear to be bullied to
" do even that which is right. And the
" matter; because yourselves, by your
" unprincipled advice, have previously
" taken away the only just ground of ap-
" plication. Instead of augmenting, it
" is now my duty to diminish his royal
" highness's income. The station of a
" private gentleman demands only the
" support of a private gentleman. When
" his royal highness shall *first* have re-
" sumed the station to which he is born,
" and which the affectionate wishes of all

2   " men

" men confpire to fee him occupy; I
" fhall *then* acknowledge it to be my duty
" to advife, if neceffary, what I doubt
" not his majefty will prevent by accord-
" ing of his own free grace (whence all
" acts of royal favour fhould proceed or
" appear to proceed) a more fuitable
" provifion for the heir apparent to the
" throne."

Inftead of any thing like this, what
conduct does report attribute to the minifter? A compromife. And what compromife? We will pay your debts; we
will compleat Carlton Houfe; but the
fituation of national affairs will not permit an augmentation of your income
—UNTILL you are *married* *.

UNTILL

---

* A later report has ftated the Minifter as receding
from this ill placed parfimony: either aware that the
payment of debts could not be juftified without a fu-

UNTILL you are married !

For many years paſt I have not been able in its meaſures to recognize my country; nor have known whither to direct my eyes to diſcover that which once was England. What a picture of mean-

---

ture increaſe of income; or becauſe all other terms were very properly rejected. At the ſame time it is but juſt to remark upon this laſt report, that although (thanks to the meaſures purſued by his majeſty's late miniſters) a hundred thouſand a year *now* for the prince of Wales would not be equal to what fifty thouſand a year was formerly; yet in the very ſame year in which the chancellor's brother, without any pretenſions or exertion, has obtained the biſhopric of Durham with its income and patronage, his majeſty's eldeſt ſon, our future ſovereign, has with the utmoſt difficulty and ſtruggle obtained only ten thouſand a year without any patronage. And though the royal eagle is ſurely " of more value than many ſparrows ;" yet, compare their income and patronage, and you will not find any decent proportion kept between the ſituations of a prince of Wales and the family even of a Thurlow.

nefs

nefs and degeneracy does this report exhibit! Adminiſtration and oppoſition con-
curring in nothing, but unbluſhingly to
palm a falſehood on the world! But
ſuch is the conſequence of a government whoſe principle is corruption. For
as " one deep calls another," ſo amongſt
political ſhufflers, one trick is met and
anſwered by another: whilſt truth and
honour and juſtice are loſt ſight of in the
ſtruggle.

If report is to be truſted, the conduct
on neither ſide will bear the honeſt rea-
ſoning of a plain mind.—You will not
augment the income? You think it then
ſufficient. If ſufficient, the debts ſhould
not have been contracted. If they ſhould
not have been contracted, they ſhould not
be paid.—Is there any thing defective in
this ſhort argument? Perhaps not; but
it is too rigorous: it ſuits better the coldnefs

nefs of a judge, than the affection of a parent. I think fo too. But his majefty was a *fon* before he was a *Father*. And the fituation of national affairs at his acceffion was fomething different from what it is at prefent. Report therefore may fay what it pleafes; but until the honeft creditors of Frederick Prince of Wales, (after a period of near forty years) are *fairly fatisfied*; I will not believe that minifters, regardlefs of juftice and his majefty's character, have any ferious intention, as a momentary expedient for themfelves, to difcharge the debts of his prefent royal highnefs.

I have reafoned thus fairly on reports, which however I do not believe. But the readinefs with which the public have received them, fhews plainly that they agree with me that both parties are capable, at leaft, of the conduct imputed to them.

them. Would to God, that his majesty and his royal highness were as well convinced of the same: and as deeply impressed as I am, that neither of them will ever be faithfully or honourably served by their respective professed adherents, unless their lives are cemented by a cordial and affectionate concurrence of sentiments; and that even a suspicion of disunion between them will ever be the signal for infidelity in every creature about them. More *serious* mischief has already proceeded from it, than those who are most nearly concerned in it can suspect: and every succeeding year will increase the mischief; and disturb the repose and tranquility of those seasons which *naturally* are, and *politically* ought to be, the calmest. I mean the important seasons of the rising and setting sun.

F I N I S.

www.ingramcontent.com/pod-product-compliance
Lightning Source LLC
Chambersburg PA
CBHW021426090426
42742CB00009B/1272